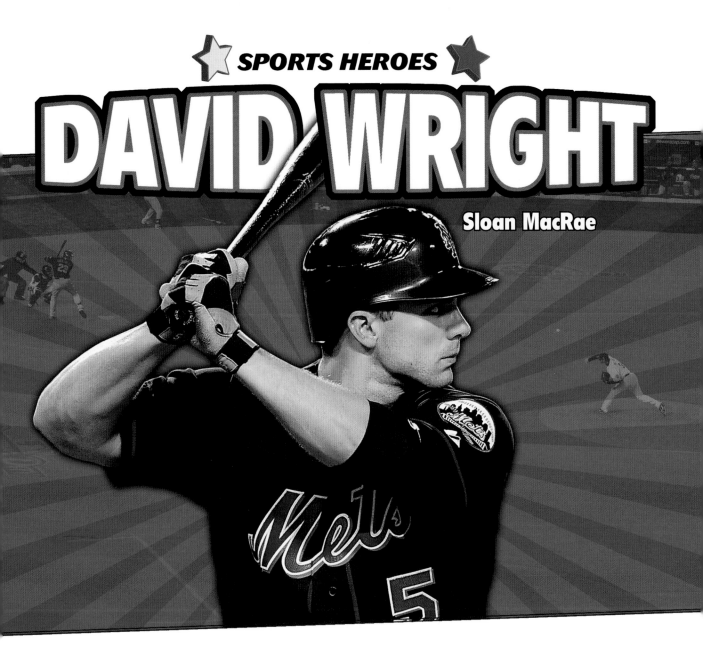

SPORTS HEROES

# DAVID WRIGHT

Sloan MacRae

**PowerKiDS**
press™

New York

Published in 2012 by The Rosen Publishing Group, Inc.
29 East 21st Street, New York, NY 10010

First Edition

Editor: Jennifer Way
Book Design: Julio Gil

Photo Credits: Cover, pp. 5, 12 Lisa Blumenfeld/Getty Images; cover (background), p. 15 Nick Laham/Getty Images; p. 4 Damian Strohmeyer/Sports Illustrated/Getty Images; pp. 6–7 Amy Sussman/Getty Images; p. 8 Scott Wintrow/Getty Images; p. 9 Joe Kohen/WireImage/Getty Images; pp. 10–11 Brian Bahr/Getty Images; pp. 13, 16 Jim McIsaac/Getty Images; p. 14 Hunter Martin/Getty Images; p. 17 (left) Jamie Squire/Getty Images; p. 17 (right) Mark Cunningham/MLB Photos via Getty Images; pp. 18–19 Peter Kramer/Getty Images; p. 20 Charles Eshelman/FilmMagic/Getty Images; p. 21 KMazur/WireImage/Getty Images; p. 22 Al Bello/Getty Images.

Library of Congress Cataloging-in-Publication Data

MacRae, Sloan.
 David Wright / by Sloan MacRae. — 1st ed.
     p. cm. — (Sports heroes)
 Includes index.
 ISBN 978-1-4488-6164-4 (library binding) — ISBN 978-1-4488-6286-3 (pbk.) — ISBN 978-1-4488-6287-0 (6-pack)
 1. Wright, David, 1982– —Juvenile literature. 2. Baseball players—United States—Biography—Juvenile literature. I. Title.
 GV865.W74M33 2012
 796.357092—dc23
 [B]
                                    2011025273

Manufactured in the United States of America

CPSIA Compliance Information: Batch #WW12PK: For Further Information contact Rosen Publishing, New York, New York at 1-800-237-9932

# CONTENTS

| | |
|---|---|
| Hard Work Pays Off | 4 |
| Little League | 6 |
| Almost an Engineer | 8 |
| Minor Leagues | 10 |
| The Mets | 12 |
| Mistakes at Third Base | 14 |
| The 30-30 Club | 16 |
| The David Wright Foundation | 18 |
| Hard Work off the Field | 20 |
| Fun Facts | 22 |
| Glossary | 23 |
| Index | 24 |
| Web Sites | 24 |

David Wright is one of the hardest workers in **Major League Baseball**. He is also one of the best hitters in the game. Wright plays third base for the New York Mets, but fans love him for his hitting.

David was born a great **athlete**. It takes hard work to remain on top, though. Wright is at the baseball

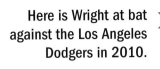

field even when he is not playing. He practices for hours. Other players see how hard Wright works, and they try to be like him. This makes Wright a great leader. It also makes the Mets a better team.

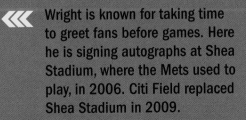

Wright is known for taking time to greet fans before games. Here he is signing autographs at Shea Stadium, where the Mets used to play, in 2006. Citi Field replaced Shea Stadium in 2009.

5

David Wright was born on December 20, 1982, and he grew up near the city of Norfolk, Virginia. He has three brothers. Baseball was very important to the Wright family. David's father was a police officer in Norfolk. His job kept him very busy, but he still saw most of his sons' baseball games.

Wright (left) is such a popular player that he got his own wax figure (right) at Madame Tussauds in New York City. Mr. Met, the Mets' mascot, stands between the real Wright and the wax one.

David began playing baseball at a young age by joining a **Little League** team. He made friends with a boy named B. J. Upton. He would also go on to be a famous baseball star, playing for the Tampa Bay Rays. Wright and Upton are good friends to this day.

David did not want to be a **professional** baseball player when he was growing up. He was a very good student and got excellent grades. He wanted to be an **engineer**. However, David played on his high-school baseball team. He loved it so much that he decided to make baseball an important part of his life.

Wright does baseball-related activities at events when he is off the field. Here he is at a batting contest called Homers on the Hudson, in New York City, in 2008.

David worked hard to become a better player. Soon he was one of the best young ballplayers in the country. He was even voted Virginia's All-State Player of the Year during his senior year in 2001. He decided to be a baseball player instead of an engineer.

Wright gets to meet other celebrities when he goes to special events. He met David Cook (left), winner of the seventh season of *American Idol*, at an event for Wright's organization, the David Wright Foundation, in 2008.

# ☆ MINOR LEAGUES

Many **scouts** watched David play in high school. He chose not to go to college because the New York Mets wanted him to start playing right away. This hardly ever happens. Most top **prospects** have to prove themselves by playing baseball in college.

The minor-league teams Wright played for were the St. Lucie Mets, the Binghamton Mets, and the Norfolk Tides. Here he is in 2004 playing for the US team at the All-Star Futures Game. This is a game played between top American minor-league players and players from other countries.

The Mets put Wright on the St. Lucie Mets, which is a Mets **minor-league** team. Baseball players train in the minor leagues to get ready for baseball's top level, the MLB. Wright played well in the minor leagues, where he played from 2001 until 2004. One of the teams he played for was the Norfolk Tides. This allowed him to live close to his family.

The Mets gave Wright his chance to play in the majors on July 21, 2004. Even great players are often too nervous to play well in their first major-league games. Wright was ready, though. He hit his first major-league home run in just his fifth game with the Mets!

Wright had a .293 batting average in his rookie, or first, season. Wright has gotten even better as a hitter as his career has continued.

By the end of his first season, Wright was the best hitter on the team. He also became one of the team's leaders. Even though Wright played well, the Mets finished the 2004 season with a losing record. Mets fans were excited about their new star. They could not wait to see what he would do next season.

The Mets' record during Wright's first year on the team was 71 wins and 91 losses. This was a disappointing record, but fans hoped Wright would help the team improve.

Wright played even better in his second season, in 2005. The Mets had great pitchers, and Wright's batting helped score lots of runs. His **batting average** was excellent. A good batting average is about .280 or better, and Wright's was .306. Very few players finish a season batting above .300.

Wright worked hard to improve his fielding skills after he struggled in his second season. Here he is during a 2011 game, after getting an opposing player out.

Baseball is more than just hitting, though. Star players also need to be great at their **positions**. Wright needed to work on his **defense**. He made lots of errors at third base. Errors are mistakes like failing to catch balls or making bad throws. Once again, Wright knew that the key to improving was hard work.

Wright won a Gold Glove in 2007 and 2008 for his skills as a third baseman. Each year, this award is given to the best player in each of the fielding positions in the National League and American League.

# THE 30-30 CLUB

Wright won a Silver Slugger award for his batting skills as a third baseman in 2007 and 2008. These are the same years he won Gold Gloves.

It does not matter how many home runs a player hits if he makes too many errors in the field. Wright's hard work and practice

paid off. By 2007, his fourth season, his **fielding** had improved so much that he won a Gold Glove. This is an award for playing well in the field. His **offensive** play was as good as ever.

Wright (second from right) was picked for the All-Star Team every year between 2006 and 2010. This is a game in which the best MLB players are chosen to play in a special game. Here he is during the 2009 All-Star Game.

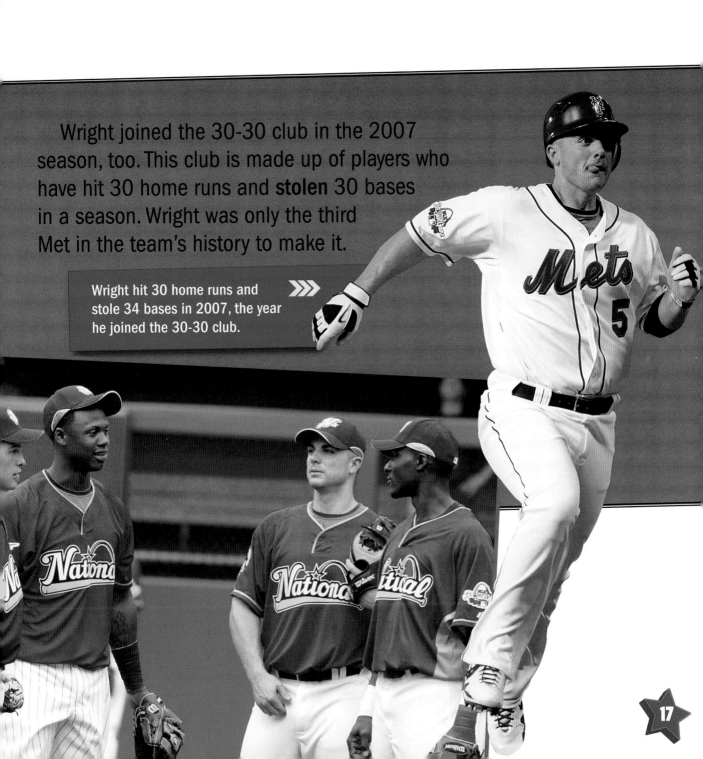

Wright joined the 30-30 club in the 2007 season, too. This club is made up of players who have hit 30 home runs and **stolen** 30 bases in a season. Wright was only the third Met in the team's history to make it.

Wright hit 30 home runs and stole 34 bases in 2007, the year he joined the 30-30 club.

# THE DAVID WRIGHT FOUNDATION

Wright believes strongly in helping others. In 2005, he started a **charity** called the David Wright Foundation. This is an organization that helps children in need. These children might be poor, or they might be ill. They might live in dangerous neighborhoods or go to failing schools.

The David Wright Foundation has a yearly event called Do the Wright Thing to raise money. Here is Wright at the 2006 event, signing a portrait of him done by the artist Marco.

The foundation works hard to raise money to help these children. Sometimes the David Wright Foundation holds bowling parties, at which kids get to bowl with Wright! The foundation helps children who live near Wright's new home in New York and his hometown of Norfolk.

It is important to Wright that his foundation continue to grow so that it can help more people. He often works with the Make-A-Wish Foundation, too. This is an organization that makes wishes come true for very sick children.

Wright also raises money for police officers. David's father was a police officer, so he knows that the work

Here is Wright with Michael J. Fox (right) at an event for the Michael J. Fox Foundation. This foundation raises money to find a cure for an illness called Parkinson's disease, which Fox lives with.

is difficult and dangerous. Some athletes get in trouble off the field. They might think they can get away with breaking laws or behaving badly because they are famous. Wright is not like them. He works just as hard off the field as he does for the Mets.

The Mets and the New York Yankees are rivals. Yankee Derek Jeter (right) and Wright teamed up for an event to raise money for Jeter's charity, the Turn 2 Foundation. This foundation encourages kids to stay away from drugs and alcohol.

# ★ FUN FACTS

>>> David enjoys playing Ping-Pong and poker with his brothers.

>>> He has a dog named Homer. Homer is a boxer.

>>> The Mets were one of David's favorite teams growing up. Playing for them now is a dream come true.

>>> In 2010, the Mets opened a new ballpark, called Citi Field. Wright was the first Met to hit a home run there.

>>> Wright was voted to play in his first All-Star Game in 2006. This is a special game in which only the very best players in Major League Baseball get to play.

>>> Wright holds the record for the most doubles hit by a Met.

>>> Wright shows up early for games so that fans get a chance to talk to him.

>>> Delta Air Lines named an airplane for David Wright. This is because he has the same last name as Orville and Wilbur Wright, the brothers who invented the airplane.

>>> Wright appeared on the television show *Celebrity Apprentice* and bought lots of hot dogs from one of the teams on the show.

# GLOSSARY

**athlete** (ATH-leet)  Someone who takes part in sports.

**batting average** (BA-ting A-veh-rij)  A number that measures how good a hitter is. It is the number of hits divided by at bats.

**charity** (CHER-uh-tee)  A group that gives help to the needy.

**defense** (DEE-fents)  When a team tries to stop the other team from scoring.

**engineer** (en-juh-NEER)  Masters at planning and building engines, machines, roads, and bridges.

**fielding** (FEELD-ing)  Catching or picking up a hit ball in baseball.

**Little League** (LIH-tel LEEG)  A group of baseball teams for kids 8 to 12 years old.

**Major League Baseball** (MAY-jur LEEG BAYS-bawl)  The top group of baseball teams in the United States.

**minor-league** (MY-nur-leeg)  A group of teams on which players play before they are good enough for the next level.

**offensive** (O-fent-siv)  Playing in a way in which you try to score points.

**positions** (puh-ZIH-shunz)  The roles that baseball players have in the field.

**professional** (pruh-FESH-nul)  Someone who is paid for what he or she does.

**prospects** (PRO-spekts)  Very good young players who are likely to play in the major leagues.

**scouts** (SKOWTS)  People who help sports teams find new, young players.

**stolen** (STOH-len)  Successfully ran to the next base while the pitcher was throwing the ball to home plate.

# INDEX

**A**
athlete(s), 4, 21

**B**
baseball, 4, 6, 8, 10, 15, 22
brothers, 6, 22

**C**
children, 18, 20

**E**
errors, 15–16

**F**
family, 6, 10
fans, 4, 13, 22
father, 6, 20
field, 5, 16, 21–22

**G**
game(s), 4, 6, 12, 22

**H**
hitter(s), 4, 13
home run(s), 12, 16–17, 22

**L**
leader(s), 5, 13

**M**
Major League Baseball
    (MLB), 4, 10, 22

**N**
New York Mets, 4–5, 10,
    12–14, 21–22
Norfolk, Virginia, 6, 18

**O**
organization, 18, 20

**P**
police officer(s), 6, 20

**R**
record, 13, 22

**S**
school(s), 10, 18
season, 13–14, 16–17
star, 6, 13

**T**
Tampa Bay Rays, 6
team(s), 5–6, 8, 10, 13, 22
third base, 4, 15

# WEB SITES

Due to the changing nature of Internet links, PowerKids Press has developed an online list of Web sites related to the subject of this book. This site is updated regularly. Please use this link to access the list:
www.powerkidslinks.com/hero/wright/